Copyright © by Lon S. Safko

All rights reserved. No part of this book may be used or reproduced by any means, graphic, electronic, or mechanical, including photocopying, recording, taping or by any information storage retrieval system without the written permission of the publisher except in the case of brief quotations embodied in critical articles and reviews.

Printed in the United States of America

This book was created using 100% recycled electrons

No animals were harmed in the making of this book

This book is dolphin safe

Generational Marketing
Communication Has Dramatically Changed

The days of being excited and celebrating "social media" has run it course. Over the past decade plus, social media came into it's own as the leading way to communicate for sales, customers service, transactional, spam, and for personal connection.

Over the past three years, social media has become less and less effective as a communication tool. Using digital tools today has become much more complicated than ever before. Just having a Facebook page, a profile on LinkedIn, or sending out a few tweets no longer cuts it.

The problem is content overload. Everyone is talking and nobody is listening. I blame the problem in part on Google and the remainder on the human condition, narcissism.

On February 3rd, 2011, Google launched it's first and most dramatic changes in the way search engines (all), search the Internet. Then on April 24, 2012, Google released Penguin and again on September 26, 2013, Google released Hummingbird, which put the final nails in our web search coffin.

Each of these changes required we, businesses and business people to flood the internet with our content. The more (high quality) content we have associated with our companies, the higher we were pushed up on the search engines. Higher rankings translates to higher revenue. It became a content frenzy.

The second problem became the decade of the narcissist, the "selfie". Today's technology is designed to promote the individual, whether it's "I'm having a smoothie for breakfast." tweet or post, or a "hey look at me!" Instagram photo, or a Be sure to watch me live on Facebook", live video. Everyone is obsessed with creating personal and business content being poured onto the Internet.

Today's Consumer
Today's consumer is more of a "pro-sumer" than a "con-sumer". They are hyper-educated about their favorite brands and products. They know where to purchase their "selfie-sticks" at the lowest price and shortest delivery time. We marketers and customer service people could only talk about 20 years ago, was building brand loyalty and building a relationship with our customers. Customers no longer care about web sites and relationships, they know what they want and how to find it at the fastest and cheapest price.

Before social media (digital communication), marketing and CRM was simply managing a bank of 800 numbers and opening some U.S. Mail. Today we are expected to manage dozens of platforms from Facebook to Instagram, Twitter to Snapchat, YouTube to email, telephone to snail mail, all in real time with immediate responses.

Now most customers don't want a "relationship". They care about maintaining their own personal relationships. They don't want to talk on the phone, go to a web site to search around, or they certainly aren't mailing a letter any more. They want answers and they want them now. They also expect to use the technology they are most comfortable with.

Micro-Segmentation
There has been a substantial segmentation in our customer base and the way they communicate. Our once easy to categorized customer is now split up between different technology platforms, time zones, county preferences, and age groups.

We must understand that, we have moved past generically praising social media as it has stopped working and has become ineffective as a communication tool. Our responsibility now, is to understanding every age group, every tool, everywhere and measure each form of communication to determine what's working and what isn't for us. I created a video to explain this: https://www.youtube.com/watch?v=DqMjHaX59dQ

Communication Through The Ages

Here's a personal example: My son is 45, daughter 42, and youngest daughter is 32. My wife and son have never opened Snapchat or Facebook. They have no interest whatsoever. They talk on the phone. She calls, leaves a message, he calls back. Like the good old days.

My wife calls the 42 year old daughter and always gets her voicemail. She never returns my wife's calls. This infuriates my wife. My wife keeps calling until she finally gets her on the phone and asks (loudly), why don't you return my messages! She answers: "If you want me to call you back, you have to text me to tell me you called me and left a voicemail." That's when my wife looses it. My youngest daughter just let her voicemail and email fill up until they both shut off. She will only respond to text messages.

This may sound like a funny family anecdote, but this is the way people are choosing different platforms to communication on.

The Generational Gaps

Studying the behavioral patterns of different generational categories can sometimes be as accurate as trying to develop a communication plan based on the twelve astrological signs. There are many generalizations that can be assumed. Here's a test of how well you know the different categories.

Can you define: The Silent Generation, Traditionalists, The Moral Authority, Radio Babies, The Swing Generation, The Forgotten Generation?

Do you know how to communicate with the: The Me Generation, Boomers, and Baby Boomers? What's the best way to communicate with the: Gen X, Xers, The Doers, Post Boomers, Slackers, Baby Busters, The 13th Generation?

What platforms do the: Gen Y, Generation Next, Echo Boomers, Chief Friendship Officers, Nexters, and 24/7's prefer?

Are the: Generation Z, Globals, Post-Millennials, Generation D, Digital Natives, Generation Like, the Selfie Generation, The Rainbow Generation, Homelanders, and The 9/11 Generation on Facebook?

Would the: TwoKays, 2K's, Y2Ks, The Conflict Generation, Generation i, iGeners, iGens, The N-Gen, @generation, Screeners, The Swipe Generation, Tweennials, and Tweens, read a tweet?

Have you even heard of the DINKS, The Sandwich Generation, The Club-Sandwich Generation, The Jigsaw Family, Boomerang Kids, Middle Age

(Midlife), Middle Youth, Adultescent, Downager, Quarterlife Crisis, Waithood, and Grey Nomads?

Every one of these groups communicate using different tools, at different times, and in different languages. And... The millennials are a whole other story! They are making a larger and larger impact every day. OMG! That's a whole other presentation. I have a more detailed explanation of these generational categories on my blog at: http://bit.ly/2iecYfJ

Geographical Differences
If you market, sell, or support outside of the United States you need to be aware of the subtle differences in preferences in communication technology. As an example, in Asia and India (I know they are considered both Asia, but the cultures and communication preferences are significantly different), WhatsApp is HUGE! Not so much here in the U.S. But why the difference.

Specifically in India, nearly 90% of all transactions are done with cash. There are no credit cards to speak of, no one has a car loan or a home mortgage, it's cash. So goes the cellphone, cash. The Indians pay for their SimCards by the month. They don't have contracts they pay each month or do they don't have cellphone plans. No plans, no data plans. They have to pay for each separate text message.

In walks "WhatsApp" with free text messaging, and it becomes an instant success. With our data plans here in the U.S., sending text is inconsequential, so we don't need the app.

In China the gloves are off! There is no Facebook, Twitter, Instagram, or YouTube.. I don't mean it isn't popular. Every western social media platform is blocked. It's blocked! They do have WeChat (微信; Wēixìn), RenRen (人人; rén rén), Weibo (微博; Wēibó), Youku Tudou (优酷土豆; Yōukù tǔdòu), DianPing (大众点评; dà zhòng diǎn píng), and DouBan (豆瓣; dòu bàn).

When I was teaching in Shanghai, I paused in front of the class, pondered, and said "2,000 years ago you guys built the Great Wall of China. Today, you built the Great Firewall of China!" I thought for sure the Chinese military would burst into the classroom and cart me off to places unknown, but they just laughed.

Now, this example might be a bit extreme, but were you aware of these? Even though you are a professional communicator?

Cyber-Surveillance
Cyber-Surveillance is more critical than ever. Cyber-Surveillance of brand monitoring is becoming much

more difficult to effectively maintain even with the latest monitoring tools. We are now expected to communicate over a very wide list of technologies and platforms and we are expected to respond immediately.

Those of us in customer service are required to intensely monitor every conversation being held worldwide that involve our products and our brands. The additional problem we face is that often within the corporate flowchart. This type of monitoring often falls into the Marketing silo. Participating in that conversation, using every available technology, measuring results and activity, identify the best tools for communicating to your specific customers becomes even more difficult.

Technology Is Changing The Human Condition
In May of 2015, Time Magazine published an article about a study performed by Microsoft about the new, human attention span. For the very first time ever, the human attention span tested lower (shorter) than that of a goldfish. Yes, a goldfish has a longer attention span than do we. http://ti.me/1A2jCJd

The study showed in the year 2000, the gold fish tested with an attentions span of 9 seconds, while humans tested out at 12. The test was then performed again in 2013 and while the goldfish maintained their 9 second span, we humans dropped to 8 seconds falling below that of the goldfish. This has a significant affect on how we communicate, market, support.

We no longer can find the time to read a book, or do we have time for a shorter eBook. A white paper is now too time consuming. Even a 10 minute video is closed out of by the third minute.

I recently authored an eBook with a colleague, Dr. Gary Witt, Ph.D. We studied 132 blogs written by the best selling author Dave Kerpen (Likeable Social Media) posted on LinkedIn. While the majority of blog reads were 50,000 to 250,000 reads, several of his blogs reads were more than 1m, with one at 2.5 million reads.

"7.5 Secrets To A Successful Blog": http://amzn.to/2j737r5

What we found was a fundamental shift from readers willing to read to understand the subject matter, to reading looking only for shortcuts. Kerpen's blogs with titles such as "The 5 Things You Need To Know…" or "Three Mistakes That People Make…", or "7.5 Secrets Secrets To A Successful Blog" had statistically higher reads by far.

I interviewed people about their reading preferences, what I discovered was consistently, their responses were "I don't have time to read a book or a blog, but I do have time to skim 5 things I need to know."

How Do We Effectively Communicate

So, what does this all mean to us as professional communicators? Communication isn't what it was. We can no longer try to communicate the way our parents did or how we did just 10 years ago. We cannot assume that everyone is communicating the same way using the same technology.

If you feel that social media isn't working for you, it's not just you. Going to more conference or watching more webinars about how to use Facebook Ads won't be the answer. We are all experiencing the same problem.

Our assumptions will fail. Today, we have to employ measurement. By measuring everything, is the only way can effectively manage our communication and relationships with our customers. We need to know who is communicating with us and where.

Be aware, there isn't a single answer to this question. You will find small percentages of your demographics distributed across every network. You need to determine where those percentages are and focus on the platforms with the largest numbers to accumulate the highest critical mass of customers. The truth is, there is no formula, secret sauce, treasure map someone or some brand stubbled upon that by sharing their story, will give you your answers.

Remember, customers no longer want a "relationship". They want the product cheap and fast and they want answers to their questions, instantaneously. CRM isn't about talking on the phone anymore. It's about getting answers, quickly, where they want them. BestBuy successfully proved that with their customers, and customer tech support where it turned out it was their customer's who chose Twitter as their platform of choice to communicate. No one saw that coming.

Fusion Marketing
Fusion is a marketing system I invented and now a best selling book published through McGraw Hill: http://amzn.to/2iHBxxO

The concept of intensely integrating (which inadequately describes the Fusion concept), describes how, once you have identified all of the traditional, social, and digital tools that are effective for communicating with your customers, you "Fuse" those tools together into a comprehensive communication strategy.

In short, are you using Facebook to drive your customers to Twitter? On Twitter are you tweeting that "If you like my 140 characters, you'll love our emails!" On LinkedIn, do you have your FAQ's? On your "on-hold" message, are you driving people to your web site? On your business cards, to you have a QR Barcode that links to a video encouraging people to connect with you and your brand?

To learn more about the Fusion process, you can read a comprehensive outline here: http://bit.ly/2i-HNByW

You May Just Be In The Dark About Generational Behavior

Can you define the following major generational marketing categories: 13th Generation, Me Generation, Echo Boomers, Chief Friendship Officers, Selfie Generation, Radio Babies, Baby Busters, Tweennials , and DINKs?

If not, then you may just be in the dark about generational marketing behavior. This should really help you and please remember to share tis with others.

Generational Behavior categories do have common characteristics. Each demographic group has a specific character based on the influence of what was happening in society during each generations formative years.

These marketing and buying behavior categories are of course a generalization, but many of these groups do have common characteristics giving each demographic group a specific character. How we were brought up during our "formative" years was formed by our parents, peers, teachers, what was happening in the news, our economic status as a group. All this molded us into who we are today, how we think, and ultimately how and what we buy.

Baby Boomers are more than just the largest single demographic category on earth with the largest disposable income of any group ever We all to some extent think the same way about life and what's relevant to us. These stages in our lives continue to influence us just by being near or over 60 years old, retired or thinking about retirement, nearing the end of our "gathering wealth" stage, our kids are raised, and we have more leisure time to spend with our spouses. All of these factors can determine our buying habits.

While the term "generation" is usually considered 20 years, as with most social sciences there is some level of give and take. These major categories are based mostly on what is happening in society; a war, a technology, or a major economic change. Many categories actually do fall into the 20 year span, some may be longer and others can be 5 years shorter that the typical 20 year span.

Let's examine each, starting with the earliest buying generation still with us today; The Silent Generation.

The Silent Generation: 1925 – 1945
This was my father's generation. They are also known as "Traditionalists", "The Moral Authority", "Radio Babies", "The Swing Generation", and "The Forgotten Generation".

Understandably, this generation was influenced by "The Great Depression", "The New Deal", "The Rise of Corporations", "WWII", "Korean War", and "The Space Age".

Being raised by parents who had just survived the Great Depression, and had experienced hard times while growing up. I remember as a kid, my father yelling at me "Turn off the light, we aren't the Rockefellers", and "We're not made of money" and ""Eat all of your dinner… Kids are starving in China." As children, going without made them very frugal and cautious spenders. They are always looking for the "bargain", the "deal", the coupon.

In their early adult years, they experience a World War (maybe two), The Korean Crisis, the Cold War, which were followed by times of great prosperity. This lead to the first tract homes, the suburbs, commuting, new appliances, automobile boom, and a major change in the family structure from the extended family to the nuclear family.

The best way to work with this generation is to offer them conservative planned giving and financial management tools. Establish one on one meetings to seek their advice. No email fundraising here. The more personal the better. They will respond better to traditional solicitation strategies like personal letters and face to face meetings.

The Baby Boomer Generation: 1945 – 1965

This generational demographic is known as: "Boomers" and "The Me Generation". Baby Boomers are people born during the end of World War II up until about 1965. These times of prosperity gave rise to large families, higher income, greater opportunity, but also was the age of introspection. Since they had to worry about providing for a family as much as the previous generation, they could turn their sights on fixing the world around us.

This generation was concerned about and made major advancements in civil rights, equality for women, the rights of the disabled, the environment, and technology. While all this sounds good, they also were influenced by the the Sexual Revolution, Space Travel, the Vietnam War, the Cold War and the Russia threat.

And, they also ushered in the highest divorce rate and 2nd marriages in history. Post War Baby Boomers grew up to be radicals the 60's and 70's eventually transformed into the Yuppies of the 80's. "The American Dream" was promised to them as children and they pursue it with a vengeance. Billy

Joel, a Baby Boomer icon best described that dream in his hit songs "Allentown" and "Anthony's Song".

As a result of these influences and drive for the American dream, Baby Boomers are viewed as being greedy, materialistic and ambitious. Put them out front and in the spotlight. Get them involved, allow them to find self-fulfillment through work with your organization. Offer them more aggressive planned giving and financial management tools. Appeal to their idealism Could your agency be a place where they spend their "third age?"

Generation X: 1965 – 1980
Next comes the "X". This is the second largest living generational category, which is the result of the largest category; Baby Boomers, having kids of their own. This generational category is also known as: "Gen X", "Xers", "The Doers", "Post Boomers", "Slackers", "Baby Busters", and "The 13th Generation" * They are also less known as "The Lexus, Generation", referring to a link (nexus), (not the car…) between the Industrial Age and the Information Age.

A generation greatly influenced by Watergate, the Energy Crisis, Dual Income families, single parents, and mom's at work. In addition, Y2K, activism, corporate downsizing, the end of Cold War, and an increase in the divorce rate. This created the birth of the first generation of "latchkey" kids.

Their perceptions are shaped by growing up having to take care of themselves at an early age and watching politicians do what politicians do, while their parents were getting laid off. They came of age when the United States began struggling to maintain its position as the most powerful and prosperous nation in the world. Gen X were the first generation that did NOT do as well financially as their parents (Baby Boomers) had.

*The 13th Generation refers to them being the 13th generation after the founding of the United States and the 13th generation to know the American Flag.

Generation Y / Millennials: 1980 – 2000
This generational category is known as "Gen Y", "Generation Next", "Echo Boomers", "Chief Friendship Officers", "Nexters", and "24/7's".

This generational demographic was the first to be influenced by digital media, a child focused world, school shootings, terrorist attacks / 9/11, and AIDS.

Children of this generation generally grew up as children of divorce parents and at the same time believed they would be the great generation to turn around all the "wrongs" in the world today. Millennials grew up more sheltered than any other generation as parents strived to protect them from the evils of the world. This generation's formative years were shaped by a period of economic growth and kept busy as kids. This was the first generation with schedules and play dates.

Use them for focus groups, ask their opinions. Put them in charge of using technologies. Utilize their networks, have them plan events that interest them. Act fast on what they are interest in or you will lose them. Link your cause to sustainability. "Mid Century Modern" is cool again.

Lastly…

TwoKays: 2000 – 2015
This generation is also known as: "2K's" (since they are born after the year 2000), "Y2Ks", and "The Conflict Generation" have grown up with two Mid-East wars and several smaller ones. They are also referred to as "Generation i", "iGeners", "iGens", "The N-Gen" (N-Gen referring to the Net or Internet), "@generation", "Screeners", "The Swipe Generation" referring to the swiping action of a touch screen on an iPad / iPhone, and, the "Tweennials" (Tweens, see below & Millennials), as they are growing up as the 'tweens' of the teens of this century.
Overlapping Demographics

Generation Z: 1995 -2010
There is one more demographic that is sometime used to describe Generation Z. This group was

born after the Millennial Generation, but marketers cannot agree on the exact start and stop dates of this generational category.

This group is also referred to as the "Globals", "Post-Millennials", "Generation D", where the "D" refers to refers "Digital", "Digital Natives", "Generation Like" (Facebook Likes), and the "Selfie Generation". These category labels emphasize this generation's extreme connection to technology and access to an infinite amount of information, news, music, television, images and marketing from around the globe. With that they have experienced technology, terrorism, recessions, and multicultural acceptance without borders.

And, they are sometimes referred to as the "Rainbow Generation", acknowledging their diversity; and even "Homelanders" or "The 9/11 Generation", which is a tribute to the 9/11 terrorists attacks and war on terrorism, which greatly influenced their early lives.

We are now up to date with generational behavioral categories; however, there still are several other important demographic groups to be aware of. this will help qualify you as a Generational Behavior Marketing Expert.

Moving Demographics

Tweens: Ages 10 To 12 Years Old

The term describes a demographic of preadolescent (usually female) who is at the "in-between" stage in their development. At this age they are considered "too old for toys, too young for boys", and have a relatively high disposal income as shown by the revenue successes of Farmville and iTunes.

TwentySomethings & Thirty-Somethings

Self explanatory and each with it's own demographic characteristics.

Lifestyle Demographics

DINK

Double Income No Kids
This demographic group is also referred to as a DINKER or DINKY: "Dual (or Double) Income, No Kids, Early Retirement" and as a "Yappie". This demographic generally includes a higher education, higher income, and often same sex relationships. Note the higher income, which translates to higher disposable income.

The Sandwich Generation

This demographic consists of families that must take care of both their children and their parents. This also includes people who have already raised their children and now must care for their aging parents.

The Club-Sandwich Generation
This is where families provide care for their parents, children, and grandchildren.

The Jigsaw Family
Describes a household that includes two or more sets of children from the parents previous relationships. Also referred to as a Blended Family.

Boomerang Kids
Refers to an adult son or daughter, particularly one over the age of 30, who still lives at home with his or her parents. These are also called boomerangers and Kipers.

Middle Age
Midlife, the period in one's life, generally between the ages of 40 and 50, when they experience a time of transition comparable to adolescence. Also referred to as middlescence. Great for the sale of red sports car to mean and red henna hair color to women along with other stereotypical sales.

Middle Youth
This is an individual between the ages of late 20's and early 40's when they are considered too old to be a youth and to young to be middle-aged. This group

is known for fighting the stereotypes of middle age. Prime candidates of knee replacement surgery.

Adultescent
A middle-aged person who continues to participate in and enjoy the youth culture. Also referred to as a Kidult.

Downager
A person who acts younger than his or her age.

Quarterlife Crisis
This group in their early to late 20's has feelings of confusion, anxiety, and self-doubt experienced by some people in their twenties, especially after completing their education.

Waithood
This is the stage in a young college graduate's life when activities such as marrying and finding a place to live are postponed until a job or career is found or enough money is saved.

Grey Nomad
A retired person who travels extensively, particular in a recreational vehicle.
I can go on like this forever! But, I won't.

If this wasn't enough, here is a compiled list of generational behavior categories that go all the way back to the start of the 1700's. Here's that list!

Awakening:	1700 – 1725
Liberty:	1725 – 1740
Republican:	1740 – 1765
Compromise:	1765 – 1790
Transcendental:	1790 – 1820
Gilded:	1820 – 1840
Progressive:	1845 – 1860
Missionary:	1860 – 1880
Lost:	1880 – 1900
G.I.:	1900 – 1925
Silent:	1925 – 1945
Boom:	1945 – 1965
Generation X:	1965 – 1980
Millennial:	1980 – 2000
TwoKays:	2000 – 2017

Warning: You may find it difficult generating any revenue from the groups Awakening to the G.I. categories as most if not all have passed away.

These generational behavior categories are general in nature. There is a great deal of strikingly accurate behavioral patterns that can be surmised by looking at the different groups for each of these different perspectives. While Generational Behavior is not an not an exact science, it will help find your staring point when determining each of your specific demographic groups giving you a new level of information and insights into how to effectively to communicate with each.

For more information about the author, please visit www.LonSafko.com

www.ingramcontent.com/pod-product-compliance
Lightning Source LLC
Chambersburg PA
CBHW050039230526
45470CB00003B/1355